WHATEVER IT IS THAT CHIMES

WHATEVER IT IS THAT CHIMES

NEW AND SELECTED POEMS

NADINE BRUMMER

Shoestring Press

Printed by imprintdigital
Upton Pyne, Exeter
www.digital.imprint.co.uk

Typesetting by narrator
www.narrator.me.uk
info@narrator.me.uk
033 022 300 39

Published by Shoestring Press
19 Devonshire Avenue, Beeston, Nottingham, NG9 1BS
(0115) 925 1827
www.shoestringpress.co.uk

First published 2020
© Copyright: Nadine Brummer
© Cover image: Pauline Lucas

The moral right of the author has been asserted.

ISBN 978-1-912524-57-0

ACKNOWLEDGEMENTS

Warm thanks to those editors of magazines who first published many of these poems and also to editors of anthologies which included some of my work, especially *Making Worlds* (Headland), *Parents* (Enitharmon), *Her Wings of Glass* (Second Light), *Entering the Tapestry* (Enitharmon) from which my poem *The Hill* was chosen by the Independent on Sunday for publication.

I've appreciated encouragement from writer friends including Daphne Gloag, Angela Kirby and Pam Zinneman-Hope.

Poet-friend Ruth Sharman, has my heartfelt gratitude for thoughtful feedback over many years.

To past mentors Mimi Khalvati, Christopher Reid and Maurice Riordan my thanks come with affection and homage.

The meticulous attention, helpful suggestions and support of my editor and publisher John Lucas have been invaluable.

The locus of the human mystery is perception of this world
– Marilynne Robinson

for all those who have befriended and taught me

CONTENTS

WHATEVER IT IS THAT CHIMES: NEW POEMS

from Half Way to Madrid *(2002)*

AT THE LUCIAN FREUD EXHIBITION

Head, hands, genitals and feet
are main events—he does them well.
Excess between is fleshed like meat.

And even now it takes some nerve to look
at turkey gizzard limp between men's legs
and women opening to a swarm of black.

Oh there's a buzz all right. Once at another show
I heard a woman in a hat enthuse
about a clever orchid, how

lips form a helipad for flies
which land in ruts, are trapped then sucked
where male and female parts are fused,

though none are needed for the helleborine
quite self-sufficient with its seed.
Can flowers be both gorgeous and obscene?

Leigh Bowery's back is overgrown with flecks,
an orchidaceous pink, buttocks sag
into an off-white stool. You sense the cracks

of old enamel bowls and chipped chrome taps
behind a drape. In front a red-brown rug
bristles. These genteel props

touch my eyes. Below each covering a frame,
upholding surfaces of this and that,
lies coiled, and I am forced to look again

at how I live. This cold October day
I'm in a crowd well heeled and buttoned up
engrossed with such carnality

I fear our coats might flake and tear
and eyes, preoccupied with doubt,
find bodies we'd not bargained for.

'UND SONST GARNICHTS'

(May 1992)

Dietrich is dead, frail, old lame.
No elegies required to drag their feet
for cheekbones curved like the quick of the mind,
that his/her voice with its Germanic burr.

There are desires screened so darkly, yours,
mine, which basked in her like sharks
she'd tamed masterfully. Recall
her black hat tilted like a tall story.

To have been suave in loving, textured
for different sexual weathers—pure horn
of plenty! I see that now. It's early May,
cloud holds its cry of husky blue

breathtakingly. The first tender of copper beech
is such a passionate transaction—perhaps I'll weep.
I have this one life only
and it is burning a hole in my pocket.

Erotic God, ineffable Names of Lust,
let me not stay behind closed eyes in Spring.
World is sheer silk, body a corny thing
whose filmy visions and whose fantasies—

those little führers cracking dapper whips—
stalked fleapits full of men in sallow macs,
and women under lamps possessed
by light that's lost and always somewhere else.

I fear old age but hope it's spirited.
Hunger's a hold that fills the seven seas;
I'm falling in love again with everything there is,
where else is there to fall? Und sonst garnichts.

'Und sonst garnichts' ('Apart from that, nothing') is the refrain of Dietrich's
famous song 'Falling in love again'.

WILD WOMEN'S WEEK-END?

"Come and find your power animal": the words
leap from yellow paper. Twined snakes, eyes
with purple irises are done in glitter paint.
The pamphlet names the Sacred Sweat Lodge
and items to bring, bangles and scarves,
a mat to lie on, a drum or mask.

How easily a Health Food Shop can mask
subversive intentions! This salad of words
is better than their greens. Vermilion scarves—
shall I wear those? Brush kohl on my eyes?
Retrieve my soul at the One Heart Centre lodge
in a sundance lead by Leah in peacepaint?

She, part Sioux, mixed snow with her paint
on fieldwork in Bransk, for a sharman's mask.
Victoria B.C. is much too British. I lodge
a complaint against that in my head, find words,
the rudest I can, for begonias. Soon I'm all eyes
for bangles, bandanas and scarves.

A ring of women with a rope of scarves
supports me that week-end. I begin to paint
with glitz and dung, learn to make up my eyes
so that nothing's lacklustre. Mask after mask
falls away: 'Woman', 'White', 'Urban', the words
sing into sense in the Sweat Lodge.

The mother drum beats again in the lodge—
a cedar womb with umbilical scarves.
Now I'm a soundthrough, a per-son whom words
can heal. Yogini songs, the blue, blue paint
decorating a yurt, help me let go of the mask
that has hidden my heart and open my eyes

to shine like headlamps, or the night-time eyes
of beasts, fox, say, or badger which lodge
underground by day. I may decide to mask
my teeth and do the dance of scarves,
a new Salome. Bells and body paint
create a self with no need for words.

Why not get real with a Thru-the-Mask
adventure? Paint lurex eyes, invent words
that lodge and change scars into scarves?

THE KALEIDOSCOPE

I saw it in Afflick's window
on the way to the park,
a black triangular tube.
Afflick, who'd sold me gumdrops,
my rubber Popeye
and set of celluloid dwarfs,
talked of a glass prison—
At least that's what I heard.
I held it to my eye like Nelson
and turned the lens so fast
I couldn't keep up
with the Catherine wheels and stars
shooting out and collapsing
into a shaft of light,
a tunnel of diamond,
the heart of the eye.

It took fourteen weeks to collect
fourteen threepenny bits
in a pillarbox tin.
The last one in was the size
of the knot in my gut—
but Afflick had kept it aside.
I galloped home with my prize,
and wouldn't put it away
with the Spanish dancer doll,
inside the wardrobe; I was a child
who needed to flounce.
I tucked the kaleidoscope
through the belt of my navy mac
and ran into the street
as if I was wearing scarlet.
When it slipped and broke
my mother laughed.

Years on I see the end of the story.
I have her weeping too
for bits of broken glass,
glinting little mirrors on the pavement.
Or I see us weeping for each other.
Could that be true? I need it to be so,
to have her a brilliant dot
and me a prism where
nothing is broken beyond repair,
and there are only patterns
I must look into.

THE VISIT

The paintings were even brighter
than we remembered; the familiar angel
with flecks of peacock in his auspicious wings

flared from the wall; gravity of hair
falling like rain, gold halo suns,
and that courteous offer of a lightbulb pear,

all one vast annunciation, whose colours
took hold. And, no, the curator replied,
they had not been recently cleaned.

Memories came flying; I recalled
the way a colleague once appraised me
saying "You are looking very beautiful these days."

I'd paused at the road's edge where car doors
opened like wings, surprised that anyone at all
had noticed such new love, transfiguring.

THE HILL

Opposite the house there's a hill,
a slope of two long fields up to a ridge
which I've watched for seventeen years
from the table. I've seen its neutral soil
passionately redden with poppies
or grass come lilac out of a mist.
I've heard bullocks cry on that hill
before seeing their bulk, the way
they nudge themselves along like boulders.
I've looked up to that hill,
looked up then looked away, to eat or talk
and I've turned my back on it
when the curtains were drawn.
Even a hill shut out exerts a pull—
you sense sky using it as head-rest.
In spring I've walked up a path
glinting with eyebrights and yellowhammers
for the view from a stand of beech.
Land falls away through the trees
into the valley and into that light place
you can't quite name on top of a hill.
This one has held my casual gaze
like the coin from a Roman soldier's pocket
which has just been uncovered.
It's only since leaving the house I realise
that the best view has always been
from indoors, from window panes
squared like a grid to draw by.
I've seen the authority of fog
wiping out castle, trees, grass, everything,
and then the hill come through again
like the idea of help.

MARGARET'S HOUSE

She went through a door in a wall
and from the end of a very long path
saw a house standing there
like houses that children draw—

blue paintwork against white stone,
square windows, a middling door
and an enclosed garden. This place,
you'd not imagine outside the wall,

was the presence that children know
is always there, although
a garden may be wild
and apple trees too tall.

The house had four main rooms;
she chose to live inside
that first view. Later there'd be
windows with small panes

and, seen from upstairs, a hill,
a row of trees and roofs
where chalk air turns to sky
and not the black, black smoke

which children draw.

THE FROG'S PRINCESS

That night, finding him in my bed,
within kissing distance,
I wanted to take the stare
off his face—those eyes
all bulge and goggle.
Then I saw their depth, a look
that could take me anywhere
backwards in time. I recalled
an aquarium under the sea where
I'd pressed my face to the glass
of a wolf-eel's tank, mesmerised
by a little reptilian head
with eyeballs lifting off
like spaceships that settled
into an expression beyond
a seal-pup's dopey smile
or the pout of fish—
like that of some new-born child
you swear has been here before.
The frog was like him,
but when he gulped and a mouth
smelling of weed or bull-kelp
came close to my lips
I flinched and held out my hand
to stop his jump and touched
a spasm of green, a creature trying
to slither out of himself.
I've been so often trapped
in flesh that didn't feel mine
I wondered what he could see
when he gazed into a pond;
he took my sigh as a signal
to kiss. I loved him best
the moment before he changed,
a small, crouched, alien thing
in need of a body.

FACE-TO-FACE

For Maurice Riordan

If that device for sensing and display
were re-arranged
would it much matter? Imagine
the nose, which keeps eyes
decently spaced,
split down the middle, each half
put in a socket below the brow,
while nostrils flare
where eyes were and the mouth
pours down a cheek.
Suppose eyes were horizontally slit
like a goat's, or clownish,
crossed, patched, trapezoidal—
the nose a rhombus and the mouth
occluded into an ellipse
of litmus paper
that turns red or blue
from fear or anger,
and ranges through all the colours
when pursed for a kiss or an oyster.

Do we need to show our emotions
by a flicker, a gape or a twitch?
Are we built into the skin of our faces
as onion flesh into its sheath?
What if we went down the street
with our faces peeled off
and our bodies racing
towards one another
to come as close as we can
to nerve-endings?

13

THE CAT WHO IS GAME FOR ANYTHING

Why do I fear her leap
onto the sill of an open window
two storeys high in the house?
She's a well balanced cat
but so eager to catch
whatever disturbs the air
I can't help thinking that
an orange-tip or fly
might make her hurtle
into free fall
like some daft woman
dazzled by despair.

HALF WAY TO MADRID

Not knowing the size of the earth
Columbus discovered Cuba
which, back in Valladolid,
he described as off-shore from Japan.

Not knowing the size of love
could it be we're mistaken
if we think we've reached our goal
when we're only half way to Madrid?

THE EYE-BATH

For John Lucas

Then, the best blue was that of an eye-bath
which mother used to rinse grit or styes.

Now there's sea through a glass of ouzo,
a man is mending a yellow net

and the sun is on it, I watch the way
he slips light over his redbrown fingers.

Yesterday the Meltemi drove
a clear sky all over the harbour.

A boat is moored with round, red rings
as chunky as my grandma's bobbins.

When I was eight the little glass scoop
healed more with its blue than with boracic.

Today there's a sheet of bright blue glass,
something pricks in my eye, I think it's colour.

PHOTOGRAPHER

Two hornets in a thistle, my best still;
best action shot—the mating dance

of male and female albatross
before the crew and I were almost lost

in an Antarctic snow storm.
"Unearthly love", one critic wrote,

seeing birds with wings two metres long
mirror each other's swoop and glide.

I once filmed ads. of yoghurt pots
a bored and happy man until

I read about our icthyosaurian soul,
the shivering happiness which comes

from nature. I found a knack
of cosying up to macaques and baboons,

their tender, grooming hands,
and won a prize or two.

Ambitious friends advised
go where the action is and show the world

the world that makes the news; they did—
a child on sand, closed eyes, lids sealed

by flies; a face, all ash and scab,
emerging from a burnt out tank.

I stick to meerkats, or the Asian plains
and poppies, in slow motion, opening up.

FOXGLOVES

They arrest the eye like pylons,
or, like other highnesses, confer
a sense of occasion.
There is such lineage here
it's as if their roots have tapped
the other side of summer
to make that mauvish red
resonate. Dead Man's Bells
some call these spikes
whose top buds, knuckle-pale,
stay clenched whilst underneath,
pendulous and pocked inside,
these hollow things unfold
an ambiguous beauty.
They stimulate the heart
before it's stricken.

This year a single stalk
with outsize flower lengths
in triple lines
became an abacus
of living digits.
I counted up a hundred, longed
to try them on for size
or, rather, find again the child
who knows at her finger-tips
how she fits in with summer
the way that bees are part,
confiding each speck of hair
of their whole being
to those corpuscular spots.

BLACKTHORN

I can't remember when we agreed
that the blackthorn this spring
had been better than every,
or when it was that she said
'What does it mean?
It must mean something.'—
as if every packed twig
were a sign,
like red skies at night,
or the berries she'd count on the holly.

I'm trying to recall
whether it was before or after she spoke
of her son dying,
that we exclaimed about he hedgerows'
intensity of white,
and were not adequate
with words like 'snow' and 'drifts',
and 'dizzying',
and how 'the ground shifts'
when you walk amongst it.

LARVA

I've not gone down on my knees
on a rock in the Himalaya
like the man I met tagging the bees
of South East Asia.

I'd stopped, in the heat, to watch
how he put his ear to a crack
listening for signals, to catch,
in his butterfly net,

feathered hairs tipped with pollen,
or bees, in pairs, spinning
in copulation or the swollen
ovipositors of a queen.

I thought a life could go by
without kneeling down to inspect
an insect's shins and thighs,
to know a different species

by its body-parts.
Then, this summer, I gazed
at a creature caught by the cat.
Not worm or snake

but a smooth, segmented body
reared up, on my hand, and I saw
how light came through its amber belly
and made it pearly as if

this crawling insect had a soul
not visible in egg or pupa,
nor even in the Death's Head imago
which enters any hive for honey.

SNOW GLOBE

Remember how you'd turn one upside down?
Sleight of hand or something in the dome
made him and her disappear
over and over. A storm
would wipe them out, they'd reappear,
and grin like garden gnomes,
not beautiful, not precarious either,
when you stopped shaking.

I'd like one now, six feet tall,
clear glass covering real people,
and strength enough to pitch the thing about,
to flurry them. But they'd be reassured
that they, the snow and I are just a game
of make-believe. This power
to make them come and go
is child's play, and no,
I never meant to shake too hard
my first cold globe that fell
out of the palm of my hand,
and from safe keeping.

MASK

Stone head in Vancouver,
eyes closed, doesn't miss

his other half in Paris
whose eyes are open.

Asleep or dead, stone head
in Vancouver doesn't ache

because his head is split
like a walnut.

I envy this old mask
his own glass case

in which he can survive
 a missing face.

HAZEL NUTS

Late August, pale and premature,
some lay in ruts below the hedge,
nestled in twin green bracts.
Rain or birds, the snap of twigs
had made them drop. Others ripened.
I found one sliced across the top
like a breakfast egg. I put it by—
a globe with a black hole inside.

Julian held in the palm of her hand
an item like a hazel nut,
and saw the whole world made and kept
forever. Only a mind in love
can see like that. I took leave
of my senses once, a nut-case
in a truckle bed. I keep it by—
this husk scooped clean.

Trouvaille or a trivial thing?
The more that I look into it
the more I see a hole
I can't see round. I'm perplexed;
my mind is more or less intact
but only a shell unless I find
a seed shaped like a globe inside
that nothing cracks.

Julian of Norwich, anchoress and mystic, 1342—some time after 1416

THE BACK-YARD TREE

If I should see again the tree
whose name I still don't know, whose white
astonished me when flowers broke
out of black and from the back-yard step
I saw our air-raid shelter newly lit
by the overhang's flare
and didn't know what to do except
invite Annie, Peter and Joe
across the street to come and pick—
in fact we stripped the whole tree bare
without a thought of damage done—
if that first tree should re-appear,
now I can't knock on doors
for children, I might wait nearby
holding myself like an empty jam-jar.

ERYNGIUM

Having seen its glow
giving off a blurred light
blue as the adonis butterfly,
and, underneath, a serrature
of leaves shaped into stars,
and the way silverblue bleeds
into the stem, I can grasp
why the design of this plant
dominates any bed. At a glance
you see that, like teasels,
it's not to be touched, though bees
squat on its spiny tufts
not minding the absence of hearts
to dive into. It's too sharp
for a child to use as a clock;
the whole flower's a gadget
some might gauge their love by—
it is more accurate than daisies

THE CULTIVATOR OF SILKWORMS QUESTIONS THE ORACLE

Will my silkworms be fruitful
this year, if there's drought?
Does the size of their horns
show their strength? How long
must I be absent from Cos?
Should my wife and our sons
depart for the mainland?
When can they sail?

Who's my main rival?
Will he cut prices?
Which spy advised him
of last year's fourth moult?
Should I sell all my stock,
or keep the best fibre?
Does the smell of raw silk
give my wife pleasure?

Is it true that my wife
has made up a potion
from one grain of eggs
pickled in wine?
Will my neighbour find out
I've killed some of his goats?
Which slave will watch over
my mulberry trees?

If a worm shakes its head
for three days only
how can it eject
a thread a mile long?
Does a blood-red moon
affect the moths' laying?
Will the girls have warm breasts
to hold the cocoons?

My wife is now pregnant—
has she been faithful?
Will she bear me a daughter?
What makes spinning-glands grow?
Why is it some horns
emit no hard liquid?
Shall I end up a pauper?
Is her love for me dead?

from Out of the Blue *(2006)*

THE ANNOUNCEMENT

You'd think they'd all get out
of their cars in this gridlock,

to look at the sky. That gold
won't last, though I've watched,

at least five minutest, the sunset
deepen. You'd think we'd all want

to exchange our stuckness, to attend
to the dazzle of smoked glass

in an office block, as if Midas
had taken hold and a palace

had risen in Finchley Road.
If we took that yellow to heart,

like a prayer, we might believe
in a sungod, or in a sky

caught in flagrancy, or do I mean
in delicto, that is to say the delight

of consummation though no-one
is mating there. Art can do that—

make us believe we see the world
as we want it to be—a spiral

of shine and dazzle as when
we're taken in by Van Gogh

or Doty or Frantistek Kupka's
disc, his "Form of Yellow"

seen through stained glass.
This November day has arrived

at a climax of light. Look.
everyone leaves their Volvos and taxis

and the traffic is left as cortège
to which a loudspeaker announces

"The funeral to which you were going
today has been cancelled."

I ALWAYS STOP TO LOOK

at any dead remnant,
eye-catching white in a field,
try to guess shape and name
of what's lost to bone or skull.
Yesterday I almost kicked aside
a whole brown animal
blurred among rotting bark.

A hindleg elegantly bent
to dance or run then moved
the only way it could
into memory and mind. Once
I saw a young red fox
sunbathe among grazing sheep,
upturned face a reference point

for this head now, picked away
in brow and nose, intact
in gape of jaw where teeth
held a snarl in place, gleamed
with whatever it is that bites
through decay. And a look
where the eye had been, a slit

half-open/half-shut revealed
something suddenly grown-up
that stared right through me
like a tribal mask, a sign
of what we are/are not—
powerful and pure. I thought
of breaking the creature's jaw

to pull out its long, curved
incisor, no tooth
to put under a pillow to wish,
nor memento mori, but
a keepsake one might wear
close to the heart, an amulet
against the coming winter.

AT THE BARRIER REEF

This tank of tropical fish
in a shopping mall
becomes almost a place of prayer
when pressing my face to the glass
I see iridescent fins
and all the illuminated scales
as a Book of Hours writ in water.

I've not been sufficiently brave
to scuba-dive in distant seas
but one may travel quite far
here, where flowers open and close
like sea-anemone mouths
and coral fragments hint
at the Barrier Reef.

Some days I wait for angelfish
and the logger-head turtle
while meeting the affronted eyes
of these dumb things flitting
like parakeets, or a highly coloured
thought repeating
I am the sacred parrot in a cage
show me the mirror of your face
that I may begin to speak.

What do we do when we pray
except shift the mind
into a new dimension as when
a fish puffs itself out to expand
its imagination—or so one hopes—
as it goes round and round?

If you came this way
you might guess
the mode of intelligence in a fin
or the genuineness of narrow lives.
O little confined brilliancies
you are what prayer is about.

LUCIAN FREUD'S "BENEFITS SUPERVISOR"

Anorectic girls may fear
this model nakedly sprawled
over a chair or curled
formless and fat on a bed.

Formless? Can one so describe
breasts, belly, thighs
worked by hogshair brush
into hummocks and clefts

veined by marbly blues?
Worried women (of whom
I am one) may inspect
her streaky browns and reds,

carcass tones that bring
flesh alive, and be consoled—
for here is a woman not squeezed
out of a tube, or only built up

by a knife. She let herself go
and flesh with a will of its own
took a route different from one
most bodies take, to move

beyond the physical into a new
dimension, a field of tumuli
where self and flesh become
the question you can't quite frame.

WHEN PAINTINGS TAKE OFF

I thought I saw her in a swimming pool,
at least, in a frisson of wind, I saw
water in gold-rimmed loops lap over
a swim-suit's dapple and glint as if
a pool fed by sun and the Aegean
could not contain itself between
turquoise tiles. Contain?
A sea doesn't contain water
the way a basin does but
aren't there times when everything
runs free? Let's say a painting
fluent with colour, escapes
mysteriously, like bathwater
only to appear again
in molecules of chlorine;
let's say a rectangular pool
may have an oceanic moment, or rather,
there are times that mind can see
under a skin of light a body
solvent and so lucid that
flesh alone cannot contain it.

RED

At six yesterday it was red
outside, brick house, ploughed field,
the copper beech whose dowser rod,
upturned, divined the sky. The world
intensified, minute by minute;
a cloud fierily wisped, Elijah
was caught up in it
and then a scroll of air, the Law?
a beard? a bush? What could one do
with all that vehemence? It didn't last.
The house, briefly passionate, resumed
a rusty look and the tree's uttermost
molten twigs turned grey. Imagine
God reflected in copper, then deadpan.

BLACK

I think of what's truly black—
pitch, a hole in a padlock

and, in Dorset, late spring,
the leafhang of copper-beech

dark with its own reddening
as if it knows what to do

with the light, like Monet
in his Night Scene at Le Havre

where sky and sea are black
but luminous, more so than stars,

portlights, or the shimmer of hay
stacked up in high summer.

My salad days were black—
Look at me, oh, look at me,

I'm dancing, on a parquet floor
at three p.m., at a tea-dance

the day after E.C.T.
My darling, willowy schizophrene

with whom I danced more lightly
than ever before or since,

a tunnel is only black
because of all the light packed in it.

"WHAT IS IT IN OUR PAST THAT WE KEEP TRYING TO RECOVER?"

– John Updike

Freedom, of course, escape
from the memory-trap.
Ask anyone what they remember
first, and see them shiver
with animation, or else give
a wry smile and a dismissive
"I can't remember a thing
before I was ten" as if
people who do, tell lies.
Maybe it's they who deny
or block out. Something snapped
at their nerves' synapses,
something broke down, perhaps
walls round Eden when the asp
reversed the world of wholeness,
the globality of breast's
confusion. There was the descent
into self. We may want to recover
the bliss of not being other
but find this or that fragment,
a pearly neck, the scent
of a burning bay-tree, maybe,
or the look of one's own doll-baby
in a hand-me-down pram;
first taste of raspberry jam;
wallpaper shuffling alive
at night. It's hard to believe
that, aged two, I was thrust
into a hole, feet first,
to stand in a square box,
a version of stocks,
a home-made playpen
that held me safe but held me in.
I keep trying to recover,
out of my past, not love
exactly, but arms lifting me

out, and holding onto me
then letting go. Something like that
must have happened, mustn't it?
No-one would leave a child
boxed in forever.

AFTER BAUDELAIRE

My small, beloved mad girl
had invited me to dinner
and through the open window of the dining room
I contemplated the architecture
that God has made from vapour
the marvellous buildings of the impalpable
and I said to myself in contemplation

'Cloud is where I belong. Why
am I here? I'd prefer to go
to the Rainforest's canopy. I want the mist
at dawn wetting my face as I live high,
at one with trees, their epiphyte.
I'd feed from leaves, nourish bark, and in an exchange
with sun, air and the roots of the forest floor

build a whole new universe
of tiny, living, breathing things—
love's syllables, love's alphabet translated. Death
would die, if the weather were right. Clouds build
palaces and domes; clouds come
over and over to repair what crumbles down.
My small beloved mad girl would not be mad

two hundred feet from the ground,
with only the harpy eagles
looking on. Snakes would fly down in a spin to lunge
at their prey. I'd hold my love in a hide
of bromelaid leaves, the sticks
of my arms thinning out as they stretch to keep her.
We would sip red berries from each other's mouths

and see from our tree-hut's eaves
the grand porticoes of temples
to worship love. My small mad girl would burble through
lianas and fold rainbow wings and sing.
Tell me, where else should I live
except in vapour? Dissolve in vapour, or melt
and condense, become the stuff to feed the earth

with all that is warm and wet.'
My darling mad girl only laughed
and poured Chablis, handed me a Sèvres plate
quite empty. "Feast you eyes on its design"
she said. The lid of the tureen
stayed closed. But then she smiled "Shall we start with the snails?"
Trembling, I prised the flesh out of its shell.

"AH, DID YOU ONCE SEE SHELLEY PLAIN?"

I was the only girl at Auden's feet
amongst a group of Oxford men, cocksure
compared with me, they could speak
and ask questions. I looked up
to his criss-cross face,
that mapped out skin, bleak
eyes and mouth of a St. Bernard who
reaches the mountain peak a fraction late
to save a stranded climber.
I felt at home only with his feet
in carpet slippers. They were beige,
the floppy sort called moccasins
in Manchester. My father wore a pair.
'Only connect' my boyfriend used to say.
for eighteen months he gave me reading lists
with Firbank ranking high and Gide,
but hadn't kissed me. After Auden
he took me to his Balliol room
and sported his oak. At least he tried,
fumbling on the bed with awkward clothes.
Our lips mumbled together and I knew
he didn't want to lay his sleeping head
on my untutored arm.
He needed to experiment with love,
to find himself, write elegies, perhaps.

THE SAMIAN KOUROS

Can't read his lips.
Level with his hips
I see scrotum and fingertips

which larger than lifesize
clench by his thighs
and resemble mine

in that posture
of wanting to touch … there
and there …… I stare

at the youth's behind—
two blue concentric lines
select buttocks most finely.

They could be natural mounds
not marble, veined
and cut. Underground

more bodies may lie
ready to be picked up like
this five-metres high

kouros. Only imagine
the proclivities of stone
to shape into someone

if given time. I've read
that molluscs on the sea-bed
needed millennia to build

first, their own defences
then, from their ruined shells,
white cliffs.

And him? Read his eyes—
their wide, blind gaze
outsees our horizons.

He stands as if
he knows the stuff
he's made from, his tough

chemistry. Feel flesh,
think how it's stressed
in reproduction, of our duress

in being real.
Now consider the ordeal
by fire that marble,

or rather, limestone
went through to become
granular, crystalline,

before compacted
into blocks, hacked
from a quarry and worked

into the serious weight
of genitalia and gait
of hero. He is right

to smile slightly for when,
or if he is wholly broken,
his dust will be stone again.

TULIP

Black and gold wings are inked
at the tulip's heart from which
the flower's sex extends,
light stigma and pale green style.
When petals blow wide in the wind
I imagine a red silk dress
a woman pulls over her head
to show a dancer's tattoo.
I can only zoom with a lens
into a flower that first came flat
then grew to the three-point shape
a cracker's folded crown would make
on top of an infant's head.
Little magus, an extravagant heart
shouldn't die into nothing.
I use a roll of film to hold
the image of butterfly pinned
where pollen falls, wings
like those on a child's skin
from a paper transfer,
or a negative she might develop
in the mind's own dark room.

HYDRANGEA SUMMER

"Can it be said that flowers feel?"
That vac. I put philosophy aside
when she and I were sent away

for her to convalesce from
some "minor gynae thing".
The question still comes back—

Blue Wave in front
of sea-side B and B's,
lace-caps like little hats

out aunties wore for an occasion,
and everywhere *Hortensia's*
bluemauve heads, close-knit,

shut up like a secret
that makes a show of telling—
do flowers guess

at something in the air,
a tell/don't tell dilemma
as when the doctor and our mother

sent us to the Cornish Med,
where dressed-for-summer people
strolled by troughs and tubs?

How did they propagate, those
tight florets, flowerheads
with little or no space

for life-givers to get in?
Maybe plants regret
being sterile. Consider

how rumbustious rubbing bees
insert themselves in bells and cups
and you sense the opening up of petals.

Closed ornamental heads
bobbed in the hotel garden
where she blurted out the fact—

I should have pulled their heads off,
dismembered all their petals,
torn them from their stem—

hydrangeas don't have heads
with brain cells in them,
nor scalp nor fontanelle.

I came so close to child-birth
in that doubling-up contraction—
was it the heart that shrank?—

I had almost been an aunt
that hydrangea summer.
And she?—Do flowers remember

thrusting up from roots,
dumb bulbs, or specks
flea-egg size, unfolding?

Do flowers mourn
a life not fully lived?
Can we pose that question—

ask what on earth it means
to say that people feel
but flowers don't?

A CAT CALLED BOWLBY

That out of nowhere gleam
an incalculable brightness,
animal lovelight, I used to think,

when Bowlby walked up me
as I lay down.
So many people scoff

at animal emotion, attachment
they call cupboard love unless
it's dogs we're talking of,

their lovegift proven
by a St Bernard, say,
or Argus who lived just long enough

to welcome Odysseus home.
A vet once asked me why
I'd called my cat Bowlby.

In a field, near a bramble bush
there'd been a handful of dusty fur
that yowled when picked up

and weighed less than a cup of flour;
there was this exchange between
a vulnerable survivor

and the small, abandoned core
in me, as in everyone,
that fits one for nurture.

I told the vet some of this,
but not how I couldn't fathom
the cat's adamant shining

that went beyond wildness
as if the wild can answer back
with that high voltage look

you sometimes see in humans
when you're electrified
by a fragment of an unfragmented brightness

that happens on you.
I merely told him
about maternal deprivation

and John Bowlby's books,
and how his namesake
came running when I called.

DRIFTWOOD, TOFINO BEACH

Past the coiled, tubular
pongy stuff like a pre-
historic sea-beast's
intestines were logs
the Pacific rolled in
and whitened stumps
carved by water and wind
into shapes for a naming game.
Here a killer-whale—I saw
the power of its fin—
and there a fallen horse,
long jaw to the ground,
hindleg up, real
as an old rocking-horse
or arm of horsehair sofa
that I used to ride, except
I wasn't now imagining
dead wood come alive
but seeing how strange forms are
the closer you look.

An upturned root, a head
of snaky hair, near stones
glittering with their various eyes
made sense of myth.
It's easy to be petrified
the nearer we get to a grain of sand
or gaze at the jigsaw parts
that make us up.
Hand we say, *arm* and *knee*,
as if we understand
the appearance of limbs,
or the lines and texture of skin
that keeps us inside, staring out
through two holes, hearing
through two whorled openings
the crack and pop of kelp
and sensing ourselves unmade,

our weathering down to ribs
of a boat, perhaps,
our arms oars of a kind,
their paddles split—
the shape of death
I can't quite make it out.

OLIVE TREES

For Christopher Reid

Climbing uphill, through short
contorted trees
I try to read their marks,
knots, nubs, scars, blebs, spurs—
the selfhood of trees
where wood wrestles with wood.
I love their convoluted writhing,
the way they clench something inside
that can't be expressed
though they let go of their fruits
when the nets are spread.
Sometimes you see one
almost bowed to the ground
holding onto, no, holding together
a remnant of wall
by muscle and roots
as if it might reach,
through soil that crumbles,
that dumbness, there
at the heart of things.

AT BRIDPORT MARKET

"Grandma's jewels", "Grandpa's tools"
I call adjacent stalls, although
bradawls and spoonbits don't rhyme
with paste diamonds and grandma
scorned the Koh-i-Noor worn
by a neighbour, the wife
of a Strangeways warder.

Now a stone set in marcasite
takes me back, in a flash,
to her street where I once found
rubies. I picked up every bit
of red, broken glass
whose glitter in sunlight
gave me a name seen in a book.

A child may not know the meaning
of rubbish. Shining is real
and this tray of fake emeralds
is a revelation—
women dawdle and stare
as if hearts were craving
an incorruptible brilliance.

Men inspect pincers and shears,
touch plain, wooden hafts
of taped auger and tenon saw
marked by ages of grip and sweat
and know what they've been looking for
when they hold a planishing hammer
or a brass button-stick.

I've not, for years, remembered
how dad polished his army buttons
even on leave and how he blushed
in the toyshop when grandpa,
who'd give me old pipe-stems to taste
and sips from his whisky
let me turn down a doll

for a Meccano set.
How does a girl fit into being
a woman? Suppose I now choose
calipers made with male precision
to measure the inside of holes,
I still could not assess
the gap between past and present,

or the point of overlap
between men and women
when he wants a sequined dress
and she a grease-gun with nipples.

BEAMINSTER

Imagine this, a town
with tower and bells that tell
time to go away.
Why else should bells ring out
so many times, or play
such different chimes
to sound a wake-up call?

Imagine this, a town
that when time misbehaves,
going too fast or slow,
or stopping dead, stays
vertical, is reconciled
to sky whose moon and sun
break through stone.

Imagine this, a town
with pitch of roofs as though
one tucks another in
while houses hunker down,
sound as a bell since cracks
and holes in walls let through
the flowering red all-heal.

Imagine this, a town
with many-sided square
and view of hills and trees
that lose their leaves but keep—
since they are rooted deep—
the shape of things to come.
Imagine Beaminster,

a country town whose clock
and bells, and golden cockerel
on her tower betray
winds of change as weather
passing to other parts
while she maintains
a dream of peace and calm.

THE PIANIST

It wasn't the way they danced
that evoked Pavlova
but their balletic stance
at the finale, at the very end
of a piece by Schubert
when fingers pointedly stood
on the keys of the baby-grand
as if not to stop the sound
but to hold back the silence
waiting in the instrument's black lid.

That slenderness, no
that largesse of gesture
turned something round
in my head. Imagine
a swan's glissade on a lake,
then, white body gone,
its resonance, a wake
expanding into an intimation—
that huge acceptance water makes
when closing over
a feathered fingertip disturbance.

SKIES

Something's missing, I think the day
lives somewhere else,
the sky will not stay put.
There is a hint of wings
in shifts of downy light,
appearances which don't arrive, although
absence is an angel of a kind.
Why otherwise articulate, or try
colours which scud,
whose names change all the time?
If I were able to keep up,
pay more attention to
the nuances of blue and green,
I could just make them fast enough
to stay. Not knowing the right praise
might mean they float away,
or harden into that one blank stare
some skies late winters have,
which do not know at all
what on earth you want
and do not care.

THE SILVER WINE-CUP

Shaped like an upturned bell
and the height of my thumb,
my wine-cup out of Russia
is an heirloom belonging to
the silver blood-line
of sacred vessels, precious
since forensic skill
might retrieve DNA
if the stain inside
contains a drop of spittle.

Not that I'll now discover
Grandma's maiden name
or mother's real birthday
though Goddards Silver Dip
interrogates the metal
for its motif of broken
triangle and circle
as if they're cabbalistic signs
and not a craftsman's doodle.
Where did my family come from?

There was the Exodus from Egypt
and dash to freedom
of a conscript tailor who
in England was "Bespoke".
If this cup could speak
it wouldn't say a thing
of its place in grandpa's pocket
when he met a forest wolf
and turned it inside out
like an old army jacket.

Rather the cup would tell
the miracle its own thin lip
bore witness to at Seder
when to the cry of *Baruch Ha'Boh*
someone opened the door
and night came in and a child saw
the becher's rim clear of wine
that shivered and went down,
in the space-time of an eye-blink
there, where Elijah sipped.

    Baruch Ha'Boh is translated as "Blessed be He who comes"

from Any Particular Day *(2013)*

NANOTECHNOLOGY AND THE FUNGUS GNAT

For the first time made visible,
fungus-gnats on the roof of a cave
remote as myth. And, yes, Arachne
came to mind the night we viewed
those mites, and their downhang
of shining. Heads were spinning
thread after thread while abdomens
delivered a white day-glo in the dark.
We saw the gorgeous structure of a trap
moths are drawn to, a veil of lights.

We can see anything we have a mind to.
Do moth-eyes see the beauty of the kill?
Are they equipped for that transforming vision
which shifts in tiny valves give rise to?
I like to think that different kinds of death
are possible, that bioluminescence grants
"the brightness of the spirit of the Lord ",
at least, a consciousness of ravishment,
to creatures that can't help themselves,
helpless for light.

TROUT

If I'd Chardin's skill
to make a still-life
from life still there,
the ebb and flow
of this trout's colour,
rose and silvergilt,
the moiled black
of patches shaped like gills
with all the breathing power
black has when luminous;
if I could catch,
painterly, that spurt
of red on knifepoint
dug into the throat
unzipping pulp and slub
when I'm unsure
of spleen or gut, or what
the size and scope
of fish-brain is;
if I could get to grips
with the slipperiness
of answers to the question
"Did it hurt—head
dashed against a stone
and that last gulp?"—
I think I'd focus
on that still expressive
eye, to show
no look of horror
but the brilliance
of a mirror where
reflections go
into a room that grows
as you approach the glass.

ALMOST SEEING

On frosty days I go upstairs
for a view of a row of trees on a hill
receiving the last of the sun.

Branches and twigs are now a frame
for stained glass, the way they take on
first apple-green and then that flush

redgold, flame, fire, ember
colours that change their pitch
before pitch comes. How many reds

does black require? The winter sky's
not firm or molten but in-between
like brushwork on canvas:

sunset ends in a deepening glow
a nearly phosphorescent white
and then the trees' impasto blackness,

that drama of their seeming more alive
powered by light that's gone
and night to come

as if black is where light's action is.
And having seen with my own eyes
the letting-go of sunset done by trees

I come to Rothko's layered reds
and late Black Forms
almost to where the sunset goes.

TALKING TO MYSELF WHEN SANE

The white magnolia is out—
say nothing, words interrupt
sensation, say nothing of
the Bride of Christ once seen
in your own head, a dazzling
one-off hallucination
that came between inside and out:
or say a treehead pours its light
in buds opening up
as chalices—the self
when hollow like a cup
may be too fragile
to contain perception
unless it breaks.

WINDFALLS

How do you measure the size
of a sound that exceeds
its noise? It's as if
apples dropping knock
on earth's door, not
that earth has a door
but something new breaks
through barrier of wall and gate
into a sunlit garden
with each small detonation,
the rhythm of a clock
gone wrong, telling the time
with start and stop
the way the heart does
in the silence after bad news.

Two friends died this year
prematurely, others fell sick.
And now apples that packed
two trees are mostly picked
and laid d own, newspaper-wrapped—
drought, wars, tsunamis
all scrunched
round the firm bodies of fruit
in an exceptional September.

A half-pounder thuds down,
a muffled time-bomb
but the ground will not open
under my feet to reveal
Hades and that lost daughter
who swallowed a pomegranate seed.
Yet it's that I'm hungry for,
the taste of survival
and Persephone's luck
to have each year divided
between the living and the dead
to halve a sense of loss
as one would share an apple.

SUNFLOWERS

It's not the glow after glow
of row on row of sunflowers
in Southern France that I see
now, not the goldwork, yellow
petals round pincushion hearts
the natural but almost artificial
brightness that Van Gogh made
emblematic, no, I carry in my head
this more potent picture, the way
hundreds of flowers gone dead stand
still facing the sun, their big hearts
rimmed by withered petals looking
like microphones about to broadcast.

VALENTINE

I'm sorry I had to rush away
with no time to ask you why
you were sitting up in bed
bald as a coot, smoking a pipe,
with that grey whippet sprawled
over the duvet. What happened
to your wig? I'm sorry, too,
I broke your heart,
it was not often that pa
gave you a Valentine's gift.
Glass perched on the edge of a shelf
is an accident waiting to happen.
If you hadn't tinkled your bell
to call me upstairs again
just as I'd rushed all the way down
to answer the phone
the dog would not have gone barking mad
and wrapped himself round my feet
and my hand would not have lunged
to send the heart flying.
As baubles go I hope you'll admit
it was only kitsch,
but I can see why pa bought it.
If I can find a novelty shop
shall I buy you another?
Does it have to be life-size,
or will it do if it's ruby red
and you can see through it?
It may be a while before I come—
I'll keep in touch.

ROSE BAY WILLOW HERB

Earth has no feelings but it has a heart
that pumps the hardest in a rubbish dump,
on railway banks or edge of road,
I think this, seeing Rose Bay grow,

remembering apparent heartlessness
decades ago when a child
on a plot of waste ground saw
her first wild flowers and picked a bunch
for mother who, on the doorstep,
would not let them in—
"They'll make your mother die," she said.

The child I was remains in shock
each June/July when Rose Bay's pink
becomes the pang of mother saying "No"
to my good flowers.

The trick is always to recover
innocence in seeing this or that—
slug tracks silvering a wall,
the emerald body of a fly in sun,
a dirty pigeon's town neck smudged
with purple, the vividness
of anything even

a mother's silly cry
fraught with colour from life's
underside, as if she'd understood
a foxglove's spotted heart,
and knew the ambivalence of flowers
from folklore long dead and dumb.

But how do I learn to love again
weeds tough enough to break
through hard ground, wayward,
the way forgiveness is
when it finds a crack ?

DOPPELGÄNGER

A boy not seen for decades
comes through a door,
a double-take, my cousin's son
wearing my cousin's face of then
as if a face is merely a hook
for looks to hang onto
when parents pass on
a family expression!

Childless I'll not transmit
even the ghost of a smile
though ghosts obsess me.
One takes me by surprise
down my cousin's hallway
where my mother holds my gaze.
Growing older, I'm stricken
by the force of 'my'.
I look into an unfamiliar mirror

wondering what does it mean
to own a self or body?
Suppose that anxious look of hers
stops here with me? It is not
Clytaemnestra's death-mask,
there's nothing epic
in small domestic tragedies that happen
when mothers become ghosts
while still alive,
and haunt, when dead,
their daughters' eyes.

BLUE

Sapphire, cobalt, amethyst,
you may list the names
of shades of blue, though
words are poor ghosts
of colour's substance,
ultramarine, say, or indigo
that going into itself
which sea does in a mood
of violet/violent blue
like the purply blue
of sea-holly in the garden
which this year stopped me dead,
thinking, if I looked hard enough
I'd know what it is
to exist intensely
not closed in
by walls, trees, fence—
a blue so immense
there were no limits
to what it might do
flooding the eye
as if it meant
to enter one's lifeblood
like the ocean without horizon
that flowed through a single plant.

SPECTRES

It is archaic now to talk
about the underworld,
how Aeneas recognised
Anchises, though spectres
lacked lips and hands.
We know the dead
are bodiless,
that they're in
an accordion tune
that floats from a window;
they're a phase of weather,
sudden hail or mist
over the hills;
they are inside us
as if there's a space
between bones or in the walls of cells,
that place where we feel
a pang.
They are a change of mood,
as when you're on a beach,
the sun is clear, the sea is calm
and food and wine go down
like the treat they are,
but there is this sudden
desolation.
You don't say a thing, merely wait
till you're returned to where you are
for the leisurely walk back
to where the holiday lives
in someone else's room,
in someone else's sheets
where you lie d own.

MAGPIE ON SNOW

The image won't let go—
perched on a black branch risen
with new white a magpie,
belly and breast less white
than snow, strikes a note
on white's variations, white
that enigma of reflection—

For months I've remembered
bright striations and loaves of snow
on walls and trees, whiter than flour
or those sugar cubes grandpa took
on his tongue or those I dipped
in lemon tea to lose themselves
in orange glow, as sun does in sea.
A blur's behind eyes that have strained
to see a sunset through to its disappearance.

But I want to be clear
about that one bird in one tree,
a woodcut in 3D, an ideogram,
a text spelling out in black and white
how contrasts of light and dark
stand out and astonish
as much as that dazzling flurry
of facts read in childhood
when photographs revealed
snow's inner life—
"No two snowflakes are alike."

If this is also true of people
perhaps a time-lapse movie
one day will show
within or beyond cells and brain
selves uniquely crystalline
to register sensation,
that patterning, say,
of magpie on snow.

THE STEPS OF HORSES

I'd not expected llamas
on a day like any other,
when I was walking through a field,
grass green as always,
hills the same distance away,
nor had I expected to see
that skewbald pony
with brown patches over his eyes
matched in size and form
as if he'd never need blinkers
and could look wherever he chose.
Six irregular shapes
of brown shag, bulky
with picnic panniers, beside
two men, two women, two boys,
crossed a bridge into the field.
Six periscopic necks
swivelled inquiring eyes
and though cloven feet padded along
soft as bedroom slippers
the pony lifted his hooves and ran.
I hadn't expected to see
something meant to show
what movement is, animal,
but spiritual too—I caught
that morning morning's aerial
happening, a creature on the ground
uplifting itself and swerving
into the wind as if
the steps of horses
at last had found their feet.

VENICE, THIS TIME

Now I know what a thunderbolt is,
for, this time in Venice
in the mother of all storms
we returned from San Giorgio
to a vaporetto stop
where a thunder-clap
rumbled a shed's
tin roof, and our heads
ducked as the sky
exploded. A girl ran by
laughing, as if that bang created
a mood of exaltation.

And now I know what it is to be struck
almost dead with fear, thunderstruck
at the row we had, senseless
as the turbulence
of a wasted afternoon,
no you and in bright sun
I couldn't see the city any more
than in the first downpour
that disappeared the canals.
The mind needs rituals
to channel its flood
of disquietude,

a convention like that rainbow
beyond the high window
of our hotel, two days after
the real storm. I hope to remember
its trajectory
over the Salute and Redentore,
a perfect bridge in the sky,
the kind angels, they say,
walk over weeping
into our eyes for all our making
and unmaking of weather
in Venice, or wherever.

THE MAN IN FANCY DRESS

I came to her bed
wearing blue brocade,
a smoking jacket bursting apart
over a quiver of arrows;
I carried my heart in my hands,
unpinned from my sleeve,
but, bored, as always,
she pushed me away.

I came in as a clown,
white Pierrot hat,
black pointy shoes,
stiletto heels, click-clack,
a buffoon of a lover
in baggy pantaloons
making signs with my hands,
when she threw me out,
as if measuring a fish
that had got away.

Changing I wore
a poet's fedora, a red,
silk shirt, recited
Marvell, Donne, Auden
all rolled into a honeyball
of language, irresistible, I thought,
but she pursed her lips to ask
"What do you want from me?"

Then I burned to bits
costumes of hope and desire
and shed, don't ask me how,
flesh and bone and shrank
to nothing at all and stole
into her ear and roared
like an ocean, then flew
onto her tongue like a wasp
blown o ff course, yet,
lest she bite through me,
entered her brain, a microchip
that made her dream me
weeping,weeping,
because she could not see me.

THE CAVE

(Melissani, Kefalonia)

And it dawned on me in the cave,
seeing snakeheads and limbs
writhe down the walls
and the real dip and skim
of birds near a dome as high
as the water below was deep,
that blue-black lake
on which we were rowed
into this other world,
it came to me, mid-cave,
at the boat's turning point
round a ridge crowded
with bald stumps, stone
rising like fungi
or like shaved balls
that though I'd not seen
the great god Pan,
nor heard his tune,
nor joined his dance,
nor even viewed his statue
found in this 'Cave of Nymphs',
I'd always known a place
built-up by water and stone's
slow copulation
where flesh stiffens into
stalactites that pierce a huge
and overarching darkness.

ON EDGE

Having been on the edge
of something about to happen
had you not stepped back
into a life that meant
to proceed with or without
your consent, you stop
now and then, still
at that moment when
waiting might have become
event, had you not feared
abyss, as if you'd stood
on a window ledge before
police hauled you back,
as if danger and not promise
had been poised on the cusp
of lip and freefall.
What if you'd sloughed the body
that held you in to find
a new skin around you,
new limbs, a lighter head
upheld by broader shoulders?
What if you'd left your life
to go on with or without you,
what then?

'NAKED PORTRAIT'—LUCIAN FREUD

Everything is portrait and everything is autobiographical…

One blind eye peers
from the picture's middle, a hole
between legs crossed, not
to be modest but to show
something as bold as Courbet's
'L'Origine Du Monde', except
this woman has allowed
her shaved vulva to be painted
and there's no pubic fuzz,
no Khalil Bey, only a public
at an exhibition where
this non-eye acquires
a cyclopean focus, compelling
as Mona Lisa's eyes, or
Rembrandt's stare that leads
into depths. Where else
would a gaze want to go
even as it travels up
to a head high on the canvas,
crook'd arm and hand on brow,
then to bedclothes like old snow
under a woman aslant exposing
her openness? Look,
is this a man confronting woman's
absence? I see an aperture
that like a needle's eye
can challenge entry.

WORKING IT OUT

Undead you stood in an expanse
of concrete, a whiteness about you.
Waking, I won't let go of a dream
that could slip away. Was 'concrete'
a visual pun, a hint, dear friend,
we'll never again discuss abstractions—
the real meaning of Freud's dictum
"There's no speech in dreams?"
Where else can we talk with the dead?
Today I'm aware that I said in sleep
"Wherever you are you must find an oasis",
as if on this unbearably bright plain
I missed water and trees.
You held out your hands, palms
upturned, generous as leaves,
asking "What do you want from me
now we're together, at last on firm ground?"

THE UNKNOWN KNIGHT OF NETHERBURY

Look how defaced he is, the way,
lips and nose almost gone, he bears
initials chipped, gouged, carved
onto scabbard and alabaster thighs
by unknown passers-by with knives
that left brow and dog-toothed ruff
intact. Perhaps they did not vandalise
but only left their mark, mere prints,
to last as long as this amputee,
this Sir Anon, who seems to me
lovelier than most statues are,
at least, more real as witness to
the past's attempt at looking noble.
There is the merest hint of paw
where hound and feet should be
to carry a promise through, unbroken.

THE EMPEROR OF EXMOOR

May he rot in hell—
the trophy hunter
who put a stop

to the great stag's rut.
The curse explodes
in my head like

gunshot, not
that I believe in hell
as did St. Hubert

who'd kill
whatever there was to kill
on a bright day in a wood

till that Good Friday when
his dogs pursuing a stag
came to a halt and snarled

and looking up he saw
in tangled antlers
Christ crucified.

Hallucination was it,
sight then sound—
a voice out of the blue

warning damnation?
Or did he really see
something—animal

guilelessness perhaps,
that all too human look
the hunted wear?

Picture the scene
not as medieval monks
confined man and beast

in one lit initial,
nor as tableaux staged
by Breughel or Pisanello

too brightly still, I think,
to realise the action
not in the chase but

in the capture of a vision.
See the caparisoned horse,
and then the nobleman

on his knees on the forest floor
adoring one head in the world
fit to hold God in.

from What Light Does *(2017)*

CHASING

Chasing our lives
we hang onto coat-tails
of selves that aren't ours.

Do selves wear coats?
Do shadows or ghosts?
They appear clothed—

to be recognized
in familiar pose—
Who can that be?

There's this high wind,
gale or typhoon,
blowing us through

this and that street,
chasing a life like
a blown-off hat.

Who needs a hat?
Who needs a home?
Yet we do need to run—

to try to catch up
and take hold
of a moment of snow.

Who did you want to be?
Where did you go?
Do you know why?

ABALONE GLOSE

That gleam the sand has before the tide
its fish-skin-wet and soft-cement texture
so it stands out as if above the strand
is there a word for it in Irish?
— Maurice Riordan

Catching the sun it caught my eye
again, background bric-a-brac
in the room, propped against books.
Foregrounded it seemed to define
my whole interior with brightness like
that gleam sand has before the tide.

My large abalone's incised
with pearlescent lines, purply-pink,
blue, green, various as sea-ferns
fossilised, except a different life
inside the shell was beached on sand,
its fish-skin-wet and soft-cement texture—

light's own life, sheer iridescence.
Who *really* knows how oceans work?
This mother-of-pearl allowed a glimmer
of something immaterial conjoined
with substance, say, body and soul,
so it stands out as if above the strand

at first, and then above a pine wood shelf
animate, not shelved nor stranded
for when eyes and heart had disappeared
and tentacles had finally let go
a mollusc left an after-life of colour—
is there a word for it in Irish?

WATERDROP

Astonished by a single
waterdrop, I study it—

you can do this in old age,
wondering how residues of rain

hold themselves together
on alchemilla leaves.

Molecular structure
and chemical laws can't account,

I think, for a globule
that looks alive

with that gold glint inside
where light concentrates.

This watery eye, this clear
bubble ballooning brightness

doesn't collapse or disperse
for the minute or ten or more

I try to fathom
its bird's eye view

of dazzle beyond sun's
natural alchemy.

And I see what I cannot hold.

INKLINGS

I once saw on a white wall opposite
the taverna where I ate red mullet
a spiral staircase rise, a definite
black, graceful sweep as if

one might well climb it to the sky.
That shadow's stayed in mind
more real than metal treads
that led to a locked door—

I think I mean more beautiful,
like shadows that add life
to flowers, as when today
a yellow tulip in bright sun

cupped five black petal-twins.
This new double bloom opened
into memories and stories—
light in Greece, Plato's Republic,

that 'Cave' where I'd prefer to live
inside, back to a fire, facing a wall
while screened puppeteers go by
carrying this or that. I'd not care

if I saw only shadows, sun
could blind. A tree in mist,
or heat-haze rising from a field
that disappears, intrigue.

We glimpse how what's real comes
and goes, the possible's perceived
like our extended shadows
we can't keep up with.

SOUNDS

Crickets and locusts, fricative,
stridulating creatures
and crustaceans clicking on
their outer skeletons
communicate in ways unlike
humpback whales
whose acoustic under oceans
is the fluctuating pressure
of water's air filled spaces.

Two people talk, intimate,
yes, but, now there's hearing
loss in one, the other's voice
is irritating rasp, like locusts
whirring in long grass, while
the deafened one, in depths
unfathomable, becomes
the humpbacked whale
appealing for a mate.

DILEMMA

Leave be or release
the house-hatched butterfly
clasping thin air between
black papery wings
folded like a prayer
that can't quite say itself?

It may not want to fly,
this tortoiseshell, too weak
to flutter in my hand.
I lift it out the window
into the day's March wind—
is that a better place to die?

What is required of us
by lives found round the house,
woodlouse or frantic moth
beating against the shade
of bedside lamp where bulb
beams like searchlight?

We're not the last surviving kin
of trilobites, we don't pupate,
we're not trapped insects, yet
those palpitations heard at night
and quiverings we see by day
come close to our own heartbeats.

THE MEANING OF RED

If red means anything
it denotes heart and blood.
Monks said a robin sang
into Christ's ear
as he hung on the Rood
and coming so near
was deeply stained.

And, yes, that glow's a sign
of cosmic power—
if not divine
imbued with myth
as if Prometheus' fire's
now feather stuff ·
and his soul there

in a cocky bird
puffing out his chest,
hopping on the ground
for modest human gifts
knowing how best
to animate, to lift
winter under his breast.

And souls? They could
exist, perhaps they do,
in corpuscles of blood
of such finesse
they can't be looked into.
The robin redbreast—
how is he read?

ALL MY LIFE

"I think that green
is what I've wanted
all my life"
– Mark Doty, *At The Boatyard*

Dear Mark, I'm on a train in England;
Spring, seven shades of green
flow past the window and then
a wave of silvery green breaks

into my heart. I can't name the tree
or that particular hue but start
to see what you mean—
Seeing, like falling in love, is

this mind/eye transaction
when light taps a nerve
like Michaelangelo's God
fingertipping Adam into his life.

Once, at a cottage door,
I saw a basket of logs
where each one, veined with light,
shone out, separate, perfect,

in a new space/time dimension
I mindlessly entered. That joy
of being out of one's mind,
not mad at all but on the brink

of perception—ecstasy,
is that what we call it when
brain manufactures its own LSD?
Or do epiphanies happen

when the eye enters, at times,
a different pupillage,
as if mind set free from body
almost closes the gap

between seer and seen?
I read your poems, Mark,
and the way you say what you see
makes words into extra lenses

so the ordinary's glimpsed
as numinous. Dora, the boat
wire-brushed to its original
green, recovered a pristine

glory as, in a moment, I see,
on my way to a birthday party,
how all my life I've been
on my way to a celebration.

GROSBEC

I'm beginning to talk to the birds
when I feed them on porridge oats.
Absurd? Am I going doo-lally

growing old? I want to partake
in birds' pecking about the gravel,
in blackbirds' existence, to understand

the one I've named Grosbec because
his beak's fatter than most and a more
determined yellow as he jets down

to my whistle when I abandon words.
My voice seems to converse with a voice
that's sheerly other, his flute and trill

mellower than the shrill from puckered lips.
One day I woke anxious at 4 a.m.
and went outside to hear the dawn

sing, and for the first time listened,
to the Hallelujah Chorus
in the Albert Hall of my garden.

When senses weaken there's a sense
inside that intensifies. Not that I hear
what world is, what world does

like Beethoven writing his late quartets.
Before I die I want to understand
what Grosbec sees with his teddy-bear eye

when he cocks his head, and what *he* hears.
Does his chambered heart have auricles
better equipped than mine

to let in whatever it is that chimes
and rings true, the clarity
there at the heart of sound?

ELIZA

A golden bowl? No,
looking closer I saw
a lid, gold-rimmed,
but mainly glass
over water in which
a kitten sprawled
on its back demanding
to be 'reconstituted'—
odd how that word
occurred in a dream
the night before the vet
euthanased on my lap
my full-grown cat
who, all scratch and bite
at first, unweaned, suckled
my sleeve for years;
who'd like a meerkat rise
to peer at distant noise
or roll over to expose
belly and breast as if
world was where, in fact,
one could let go
and trust until
the tumour stopped her
from that easy movement
when she'd tease
with those yellow eyes
that with facial marks
hinting of lynx linked
her to a wild place
most domestic felines
wouldn't even dream of,
so I think, now missing
gold glints in fur,
the texture of presence
she gave to empty rooms—
even when she hid
I sensed her there
like breath waiting
to embody greeting.

SPLIT SECOND

It did not change her life
as near-death experience
is said to do—

a blip of brain, maybe,
two halves, out of sync.,
bombed out by stimuli.

First Bharratpur at dawn,
a lake with painted storks
then the bus to Jaipur

packed with people, cooped
hens, cans of paraffin,
the smell of sweat and gasoline

then, at the terminus,
the stench of rotting veg
fended off by limes

stuffed in nostrils until
she'd showered and slept.
At 4pm, downtown,

under rose-red skies
past white parapets
where black-faced monkeys

chattered, she took
a pedal-rickshaw dodging
two-humped cows,

bikes and camels dragging
carts, each empty
except for deck-ends

with little pyramids of sand.
At the road's edge elephants
processed for festival.

"And then," she said,
   this woman I know well,
"I wasn't there at all—

   but part of everything
   there is, belonging
   to world's whirligig

   of transport, as if"—
   and this is how she put it—
"for one split second

   life lived me."

NOT CRYING FOR THE MOON

I'll not fly to the moon
in future years to view
the globe's rotating hues
nor take a trip to Mars,

nor hear news to come
of new-found bodies
orbiting new stars,
but year by year I've found

small galaxies in woods
when February unearths
its first white flowers.
Or seen, in May, how light

takes hold of sea and sky
in Greece. There is a blue
to die for and sunsets
that blaze more brightly

in smoke-polluted cities.
Perhaps, we live inside
a giant kaleidoscope—
Who's not been shaken up

with patterning world does—
fishscales, birdwings, irises
in cats and cattle, eyes
of peacock butterflies?

Ilan Ramon, the astronaut,
when walking on the moon
having a bird's eye view
of our whole planet's glow,

enraptured by its blue
longed not to come back
to earth. But isn't it enough
for most of us who've lived

with mix of joy and pain
to gaze from time to time
at harvest moons, or wait
to watch the moon's eclipse?

BREAKING BOUNDS

Death was child's play
in Cheetham Hill
when I with my pal Sam
clambered a low, brick wall's
sharp, triangular peaks
to break and enter Langer's
Monumental Masons Yard.

We'd gawp at gravestones,
reading names we didn't know
deep-cut in black and gold
in English and Hebrew
not wholly aware that marble
could be holy nor how hard
it was to work with granite.

Under powdery dust
we found, once, a trapdoor
that led down to a room
 where, laid bare
in ledgers and receipts, we saw
what being buried cost.
Not that we understood

what death meant. We glowed
descending and mounting
steep, narrow steps. Outside,
we kicked a ball around;
Sam or I would stand
between two uncarved slabs
we used as goalposts.

KOL NIDREI

(All Our Sins)

A woman, at last,
aged twelve, allowed
first full day's fast,
when, in crowded shul,
I confessed
every sin in the book—
in Singer's Prayer Book,
to be precise—reading
a list in Hebrew
(translation alongside)
of each forbidden act
that in any language
I didn't/couldn't know.

It's what we Jews did
on the Day of Atonement,
one for all and all
for one—do we call
that collective guilt
when we so repent?
It's what my aunt meant
when I spoke up
for the first of my cousins
who married 'out'—
You cannot be
an individual, you are
a member of a group.

PAPER TREES

Even if I could, would I now unglue
paper leaves I'd weekly stick
on the bare, brown outline of a tree
bearing my name?

Week after week pennies paid
would build on a certificate
a tree bearing my name, for a forest
to come, something to stop erosion.

Is it still there, in Israel,
a tree bearing my name
not like a stick of Blackpool rock
or bench on Hampstead Heath,

but registered or on a plaque?
Or has my tree, worn away
by drifts of sand and desert wind,
not thrived at all? Has it been struck

by bombs or cleared, making space
for bungalows and swimming pools
while olive groves are vandalised
and thorn-trees near the long-lived homes

of Palestinians? Is he a strong man,
Netanyahu ? Look how he surveys
rubble through binoculars still capped,
eyeless in Gaza.

Would I now choose through grief
and guilt to uproot any tree
I bought as a child? Yes or no?—
For all the world I can't unjew me.

A NARRATIVE OF NOTHING

Nothing can undefame
Dreyfus, uninspire
Theodore Herzl
and nothing can turn off
shower taps in Poland,
unbuild crematoria,
unburn side-locks
or unorthodox faces.

Nothing can undo
what was done to
Gaza, or now expand
that single verse
in Genesis *And Isaac*
together with Ishmael
buried their father Abraham
in Machpelah—

Unless Isaac and Ishmael,
in Jenin, Hebron, Gaza,
come together, two
narratives side by side
relating to each other
to bury past catastrophes—
history a palimpsest—
old texts rubbed to nothing.

THE MENORAH TREE

Dispossessed of gardens, among the brick and slate
I sought a rubric for germination
in the terraced street.

It lacked succulence except for pavement cracks
where pitch globules pricked into black sap
gave children proof of foliation.

Now, seeing lawns mature with dappled trees
where thrushes sing, I recall
the occasional tablecloth rolled to a perfect finish

and my father's menorah tree bursting
into onyx cones forged
from a mix of smoke and tallow-wick.

He knew a silken sky, the white blue-banded awning
raised by prayer shawls before the Ark
when a millenial Kaddish was intoned,

while I miss a liturgy to reconcile
the ghetto and the suburban garden
straddled by my uncomfortable generation,

all dispossessed of forms to mourn or bless
the fissure in which roots still struggle
to hold, when all else dies, belongingness.

TATTOOS

There are no adequate designs
for what I want. Yet, though the act's
ruled out for Jews, I like to think
I'd have myself tattooed
all over if choosing
to be tribal, no disconnect

from kith and kin nor those
I've loved. Unlike beauty
love's indelibly skin-deep
as paint with pain from needle-pricks
penetrates to mix different hues
with flesh and blood.

Wrapped in skin containing
my only body, I'd work out
who I am, perhaps, seeing
in full length looking-glass
who or what's meant most to me,
if I could go against taboo—

with ankh, cross, star, pierced hearts,
shapes of head, his and hers,
lines of verse and scripture text
and one blown goodbye-kiss
that's every tiny space
between a thousand images.

MY PARENTS' GIFT

Who knows what could happen
to one unafraid? When I was five
trouble began; I couldn't move
upstairs to bed but stood

on the bottom step, transfixed,
as in adult dreams trying to run
down endless corridors of trains—
all those non-sequiturs in sleep,

followed, hunted, paralysed,
are they the self unravelling
a life unsolved? What is it
some children want to escape?

For me, perhaps, the eyes of God—
that blaze of blue from panes of glass
in the front door when the light was on,
then whatever lay in the dark ahead

without shape or name.
A mantra helped for that flight
of stairs. On the bottom step
mother or father'd stand by my side

and I'd say after them
words that worked then—
'Adonai lee,veloh eerah—
The Lord is with me, I'll not fear'.

SHE LIVES IN ME WHEN I WRITE HER DOWN

A house made of chocolate like the one
she gave me was what mother, in hospital,
asked for. I looked in umpteen shops
but no confectioner had in stock
such a construction, nor did I recall
her gift of a doll's house of sweets.
Perhaps she wanted a home-sweet-home,
not the war-zone of words we lived in
when her mouth with a will of its own
screamed "a chalerah on you"—
that corruption from God knows where
of 'may cholera come upon you!'

A mouth that can't be stopped may drive you
to murder. My sister once tried to strangle
our mother; once *my* hands round her throat
flinched away as when you happen to touch
a slug. It wasn't the skin of her neck
that repelled but the feel of my fingers
about to choke. I'm sorry, I'm sorry, I'm sorry.

One night, when I was seven or eight
and going to bed, she stood at the foot
of the stairs, her voice following me up
in one more shrill tirade.
Next morning, baffled by black streaks
on white sheets, I asked what happened.
She'd popped into my mouth, as I slept,
open-mouthed, a chocolate or two,
being the mother she wanted to be—
wishing chocolate to come upon me!

MADAME CÉZANNE IN YELLOW CHAIR

She holds a rose; the flower,
close in colour to her frock
though barely visible,
is there, perhaps, to help compose

a harmony of reds. Her eyes,
asymmetrical, may discompose
a viewer. The picture's angles
slow down our perception

of a wife, the way her chair
slants down as if light slips
behind her back and walls
tilt towards a curtain growing

apples. In a room that shifts
around her there's one line
perfectly straight—the parting
in her hair; thus a head's

determined, while elsewhere
oranges are on the brink
of being live and haptic.
And she is almost touchable,

but eyes betray the distant look
of someone close to feeling
nothing. Or, maybe, the stem
wedged in her fingers pricks.

How long has she been sitting
with a rose that's half-alive
in her hands.? And is this
a portrait of a marriage?

SEASCAPE

Black, huge eyes
looked right through him
as if they held superhuman
intelligence, so Paul said
in the middle of a tale
of vast proportions—length
of shark, the fight—
three hours duration,
immeasurable girth
that made him think
the Hammerhead was female
and the sheer weight
of strength required
to loop rope round its head
and pull and keep on pulling
a fish whose thirteen feet
if hauled on board
would have sunk
their twenty-foot boat
it first dived under
lured by tuna bait
then thrashed by,
up, down, sideways,
in a tug of war
that dragged the skin
off his hands
until he leaned over
to stare into those eyes
each end that mallet head
and stumbling gashed
his leg, blood everywhere
he noticed only when
the Portugese skipper shrieked
and with machete cut
the shark free
to sweep the sea
with a single glance.

JURASSIC

(West Bay, Bridport)

Though I did hear the thud of hooves,
and saw huge crests, the charge
of waves, I'd not want to use
'white horses' for the height of swell
on a day of storm requiring
something direct as the cry of a gull.

Yet, for me, one man avoided
cliché—all buttoned up
in the gale but wide-eyed,
who gazing at sea's blind
fury at cliffs molluscs once formed
replied to my "Isn't it grand"—

"That's what the sea's all about."

WHAT THE SEA WAS LIKE

(Piana, Corsica)

That time the sea wore red
that time the sea wore
ultra-violet light beyond
the luminous, after storm's
violence, vibrant red
beyond day's shifting blues
that time the sea became
a field of shed, red petals
or rather, stepping out
of its water-body
a naked glow
when sky let go of cloud
allowing sunset through
to take away
a limiting horizon—
what was it really like
that vastitude of red?—

Nothing I'd seen before
except, one time,
a bullfinch
atop a bush covered with snow
brought world into focus
at the point of the colour
of his breast—
the point of why
it doesn't matter
how we come or go
or if we don't know
the names of hues
light makes and then undos.

Whatever It Is That Chimes:
New Poems

DOORPOST

Silver, pewter, gold or precious metal
intricately crafted—now *that*
would have been worth keeping though

I'd not now fix a mezuzah
to my front door. Like survivors
of tradition I'm a secular Jew—

yet I'd no more dump in a dustbin
this cheap, tin, yellowing tube, thin
as if there's no klaf in it—

no *Hear O Israel* bulking it out on parchment
than I'd refrain from kissing a bible
that falls to the floor.

A sense of the holy may be engrained in us
from habit or superstition.
I keep this mezuzah, no *Shaddai* on it—

as relic from the first front door
that let me out into the street.
Parchment inside is worn with age—

Sometimes I imagine my body's a doorpost
telling me who I am and what I'm for
with inked text in my veins

and an alphabet other than DNA
composing my essence.
Fanciful, yes, but I'm parched,

thirsting for something I can't get hold of
which fingertips pressed to my lips would then kiss
if I knew the right name.

mezuzah is name of object affixed to front doors of Jewish homes and also
means 'doorpost'

FIRST BOOKS

The bible inscribed to me, aged nine,
is coming apart; spine, gold-tooled,
the worse for tear not wear
is cracked near Malachi .
And I don't know why he ended
what Genesis began.

The generous aunt who gave
the biggest book I owned
as a child, a tome of bible tales,
hadn't noticed both Old and New
Testaments were inside.
What did Jesus do to the Jews

to make him taboo? I was not
as brave as Grace Darling in
'The Girls' Book of Heroines'—
I'd not have risked my life
in a boat on a stormy sea
but I dared to peek at Jesus

walking on water, then read
and looked more and more
at full-page illustrations
of the man in white, flowing robe,
like Moses on top of a mountain
but then with the lame and lepers.

And I did this more furtively
than when I forced out the sex-book
from where it was wedged against
the doors of the gramophone cupboard.
If I heard mother's tread come near,
as I read about Christ, I'd rush

from back to front in the book.
How had I learned to dread Jesus ?
No-one I remember had said
I must run past Brideoak Street's convent
as if someone was out to get me.
To this day I brood on Jesus—

who on earth did he think he was?

MALAPROPISM?

Maybe she did not say the wrong
word, my sister, nor did I mishear
her telling my very young self
she wanted to be a banister.

Maybe she knew, all her short life,
all she wanted was not the law
but people who'd hold onto her
so neither they nor she would fall.

OH DE DOO-DAH DAY—

No-one now sings minstrel songs, though
from time to time I catch
on radio a snatch of Camptown Races
and, not knowing why, I want to weep.

Did something happen first time round
I heard of race-tracks five miles long
in childhood? Yesterday
the tune wormed up again.

Not being Proust I can't unfold
nor explain the past;
googling the words I wondered how
hippocampus may retain

music and feeling with no trace
of what event once caused
desolation. De doo-dah day—
That almost nursery-rhyme's

a weight my body bears
inside, deep-down. Perhaps,
for lots of us the past's a body
waiting to be exhumed

so a crime may be laid
to rest or be transformed
into bob-tailed mare or grey
and not the mare we ride at night.

IN FRONT OF THE ARK

When all the men called Cohen,
each, by dint of name, a priest,
came out of the congregation
to stand in front of the Ark
heads and shoulders covered
by one huge prayer-shawl—
their tallitim meshed together,
when all became one bulk
that wailed and chanted
so tense a silence fell
I didn't dare look up.
Unknowing, I learned then
prayer and fear are one.

I expected something to happen,
maybe a transformation
making sense of hidden presence.
But the men went back to their seats
and left shul in their tailored suits.
          How could they resume
ordinary lives, men called
to utter words as if they knew
who they were talking to
and why they covered their faces?

     Tallitim is plural of tallit—prayer-shawl.

ICON

A ridge, all black,
on it a black ewe waits
stockstill and some way off

a lamb, in silhouettte,
back hooves kicked up
head raised—

you almost hear
a bleat—in mid-run
toward her

is all movement
in a moving still.
Did the photographer

work with or against the light
to catch in black and white
this 'mother-child reunion'

in an impending storm?
I bought the photograph
to keep not send, although

I had been browsing
for a birthday card.
This captioned *Timeless Moment*

could be for me.
In and out of real time—
is that what 'universal' means

when it signifies
a wholly personal sensation
in images that haunt,

hurt and heal the heart?
The camera never lies,
nothing and every thing

happens in a flash—
we know there'll be an end
to separation.

MY MOTHER'S SILVER HANDBAG

Today I stand in your shoes
in your youth; I don't dance,
can't wear high heels,
but unwrapping the bag,

the small, silver handbag
dad gave for your seventeenth,
your dad, I, mean, not mine,
except when I'm you,

I find I've nowhere to go.
There are no debutantes
in Cheetham Hill and no
dance-hall grand enough

for this hall-marked purse
kept in tissue paper
to remain untarnished.
In a flash I see The Assembly Rooms,

across the road from father's shop
with its window's male mannequins .
Maybe I'll go to a ball
free from seven pesky sisters,

and come home in a coach,
in glass slippers, a pair
and easily broken
unless fairy tales come true—

No-one else in the family owned
a solid silver bag that bulged
to look full even when empty;
it swells into a statement—

I am a much loved daughter—
when I am you.

EYE-WASH

An infected eye? Children
don't know what they're missing
when a stye troubles vision

and mothers fail to work magic
to keep them wide-eyed.
Mine rubbed gold wedding ring

round a lump on an eye-lid.
and ended maternal enchantment
spitting into my eye.

In this digital age children
may no longer be heirs
to primaeval tradition;

and they may not still read
Lang's *Pink Fairy Book*—
of Kay whose eye was infected

by a splinter that flew
from a goblin's mirror
breaking into a billion bits.

Gerda, a friend like a sister,
found him, at last,
in the Snow Queen's kingdom

and her tears washed away
an evil sliver of glass
distorting the visible world.

Kay's eyes sparkled again
when finally she kissed him.
I learned the mouth's power

from my mother's saliva.
A mother may spit in your eye—
does it matter? A drop of hate

more than a flood of love
or the eye-wash of superstition
can make you see better.

THE SAND DUNES

We could be other than we were
on the Sand Dunes, forbidden place
set apart from streets and usual park.
On that yellow field extending from low hills
we were travellers to the Holy Land,
our feet unearthing antique shards—
not those Job sat on when he cried
to God but bits of broken crocks
glazed blue and white like aunty's tea-set.

Out of the blue a man appeared one day
on crutches, hand held out for coins.
My friend gave a penny while I
feeling deep in my pocket, touched
a silver sixpenny piece, gift
from dad on leave. 'Keep or Let go'?
Unwilling fingers forked it out
and I'd this sense of being good
until dad turned up—someone had snitched

seeing two girls where they should not
have been. My father, in khaki,
turned the man's trouser pocket inside out
and told the beggar to bugger off.
My sixpence back I felt ashamed
of being glad and not as good
as I thought I was. Since then,
as if travelling on sand dunes,
I've sensed from time to time
ground shift under my feet.

DOORS

Even in autumn a door
opens, sometimes, into a day
for you to see heaven, at least,
Michaelmas daisies vibrantly blue.

And in Greece, in hot, high summer
a cry breaks a hole in the day
when a tethered donkey brays,
unshaded, and you see hell.

FULL CIRCLE

Today thin, twisted threads
create a perfect circle
drawing gaze into gauze and shimmer
as did yesterday's web

poised between rose and hebe.
Now air separating these shrubs
suspends a light construction
perfectly woven, though wavering

in wind. It retains a roundness
draughtman's compass almost
copies. The garden's become
a place where buildings happen—

like the Salute's dome, glimpsed
once from a vaporetto,
when flat against grey sky
no solid stone appeared

but grisaille, or architect's plan
realized in a moment of
apperception, as when I saw, I thought,
the shape of worship.

Now a spider sits in the middle
of her own radiance while I
seek the form of prayer words are
if drawn out from one's body.

THE PIANIST AS BIRD

I'm never going to know
how that distant speck,
one small bird
alone in overarching sky
has power enough
to rise so high, so sure
of destination. I look
till it disappears wondering
where *she* went last night,
the pianist whose hands flew
over the Steinway's keys
making them sing
with every pitch, tone,
and change of tempo,
as sounds whose ripple,
crash and flow surpassed
most keyboards' range.
From time to time
that girl of slender build,
head back, looked
up, eyes closed
as if she entered
a new dimension,
that rare blue I see,
craning my head to watch
speck, visibly bird,
make its way to what's
out of sight, some point
beyond the airy sky.

GRASS SNAKE

A few inches
of dark brown skin
slithered near my feet,
unmistakeable
though thin and not
Lawrentian, nothing
to write home about
only to be asked
'was it a slow worm'
as if I'd not observed
how it moved
curving, uncurving, crawling
on non-existent belly,
blackish brown except
for off-white collar
where a neck should have been
below head upraised
with that amazing mouth
open and all flick
so quick, to and fro,
I couldn't work out
if tongue tried to trap food
or if the infant
was practising a hiss
or, as I looked at the garden,
it was viewing the world
with its quiver of spit
to express the venom
of what looked like derision.

IN THE FIELDS

"The Ledges" locals call fields
  sloping down in ridges
  like ribbed tops of knitted sweaters
  or West Bay's Jurassic cliffs.

  At the edge of one of these fields
  I once knelt to pick a cowslip
  near the stump of a tree
  rotted down and barely noticed

till a barn-owl flew over my shoulder
from a hole still strong enough
to house that bird wearing
a heart for its face.

Face? Or was it a mask
with those deep-cut dark eyes
that saw whatever was wanted?
Had it tried to send me away

by flight skimming my head?
Did my stoop provoke fright?
I remember sensing the hardly-ever,
a raw moment of encounter—

wings almost brushing my shoulder.

CAROLINA

Buckydoo-Square, Bridport,
four old men played guitar
harmonica and wooden drum
to us who, that market-day,
sat on benches in the sun
tapping our feet.

One white-haired man sang truly
a song with this refrain
>   *Take me home,*
>   *Take me home .*
though 'home'was Carolina
and he'd not come from the USA.

This is what nostalgia is,
that sense of an elsewhere,
and yearning to be back where, perhaps, we never were.

DEER

1

A deer lays his head down on a man's lap
like someone's dog; a carving
in St Giles Church at Hooke
told a tale I had to look up—

Starving, the monk was fed
by a hind sent from God.
And he took the bullet instead
of a deer fleeing the hunt,

or rather, an arrow
that wounded his leg; possibly
the damaged and lame may know
the depth of animal pity.

2

What was the point
of Artemis' punishment
of Actaeon if antlered head
lacked human brain
and he, as stag savaged by dogs,
was unaware how the act
of gazing becomes violation?

3

Can looking hurt?
One Christmas midnight
a friend and I drove from the House
of Franciscans in Dorset,

and from a narrow lane came
onto a tree-sided road where
two fawns, eyes bright with frost,
and huge as our headlights

stood alone,shining.
In a flash they were gone
as if unable to bear
the wound of our perceiving.

4

Painting herself as *Wounded Deer*
had Frida Kahlo seen
Christ Crucified rising
between a stag's antlers

pictured by Pisanello or Brueghel—
St Hubertus or St. Eustacus
on a Good Friday hunt
stopped in their tracks?

Kahlo posed her own face
in a skull topped by antlers
like branches that grow
from the roots of her life.

5

In St Clemente, Rome,
I saw that gorgeous apse
and brought back a post-card
detailing a deer, head down in a brook.

The psalmist wrote *As the hart*
panteth after water so my soul
panteth after thee, my God.
Picture tesserae, green and gold,

and ponder homophones—
hart/heart; deer/dear; chased/chaste.
These words, maybe, share roots
from which language grows

as the tree of real life.
Let us suppose we live in metaphors
and drink from the river of Paradise
when we remember stories.

STREAM

Do top naval brass wear red?
Above my head on buddleia
red admirals begin to feed
a stream of consciousness.

Was insect name derived from
men with medals on their chest
boarding ship like Horseguards
on parade? There's puzzlement

in source and size and shape of words.
The Greeks knowing everything
is both itself and something else—
prior to Pessoa, that is—

used 'psyche' to denote
both 'butterfly' and 'soul'
as if aware we humans flit
from this to that, ephemeral

but more capable of flight
when freed from flesh. The day
my black cat died I saw
a huge black butterfly in the yard—

Coincidence? Or, did a moth
mistake day for night? Souls
and selves have disappeared
in flow of sense and thought—

we can't step in the same river twice
but time and time again we move
into streams of consciousness,
different rills and brooks

fed from a source we know is there
like whatever grounds the sea
beyond its bed, a core
that can/cannot contain us.

SINGULAR

"Odd to be one not plural" I woke
with these words from a dream
in which an ibis in a picture spoke

with animation. What did it mean?
And was the bird, perhaps, an albatross?
I could not think where I had been

last night, a place, no doubt, of loss,
of Rilke's depth-dark sobbing, semibreves—
owls' who-who-who of loneliness.

I thought how Oscar said our real lives
were those we hadn't led.
Before sleep I saw a TV film of caves

with gypsum chandeliers and stalagmites
like towers. A camera crew
braving new depths achieved new heights—

a shot of cockroach in a mile of poo
they didn't shirk; three million bats
in Borneo then cloud-scud to Peru

and limestone canyon habitat
for eyeless larvae. Catch
as catch can—I watched a fungus gnat

dangling silk for prey and worms
abandoned by the sun—
out of the limelight glow-worms

hatch in holes too dark to imagine,
while we hang by a thread in time,
cocooned in a single limiting skin,

in chancy bodies. I can't even name
everywhere that I want to go—
There was a time when meadow, grove and stream ...

What have I done with my life till now
to match the poise of a troglodyte
filmed in a waterfall's fast flow ?

BALANCE

Mobiles, static in a gallery,
idiosyncratic the way
irregular lengths of wire
like coat-hangers suspend
circular, white discs, now big,
and now diminishing in size,
complex conceptions to visualise—
they show perfect balance
as birds do whose thin legs,
feet and tripartite toes
seem disproportionate
to their bodies
but stand their ground
landing on fragile twigs.

Prone to mood swings
I envy the engineered poise
of Alexander's Calder's artefacts,
and small, plump-breasted birds
that negotiate different weights
of sky, earth, trees
and safely roost.

OF NARCISSISM

But how did Narcissus' name
signify a state that's deplored?
Not knowing his own face

in water, how could he be
in love with himself?
It's a complex story—

pining and dying, renascent
as a god-created flower
he puts us on the scent

of a hidden truth—over and over
we yearn for that part of ourselves
we cannot discover.

THE HOUSE OF NAILS

With my unpolished finger tips
once bitten to the quick
in childhood, let me go
into The House of Nails
to have them groomed, clipped
and painted though not young
enough for dazzling shades
of green, blue, red to hold
up to the light. Let me enter
the place not named Nail Bar
or Saloon but somewhere sounding
more grandiloquent as if we're meant
to think of aristocratic lineage
rather than how our forebears went
back to primates—apes, I mean,
our hands the residues
of claws, tools to scrape and scratch
more than a living.

I imagine entering
The High Street's 'House of Nails'
to gather pared finger-plate
out of respect for dismemberments
of small but intricate constructions.
But would I inter them with a prayer?
like sorcerers who once buried them
to grow three days in earth?
so they could work a lethal spell?

No, I don't believe in magic though
at times I can almost have faith
in James Joyce's nail-paring God
standing back from the world
as if He'd nothing better to do.

In The House of Nails
technicians may be wizards
using golden scissors, silver clippers
to create heavenly nails
where small moons shine
and no-one would suspect
they'd be plunged
into the washing-up
or harbour grime.

All fantasy, of course,
But if I went into that Hampstead shop
I might gain a new sense of self
as one who could flash a hand around
fit for a ring. Or, if not that,
I would, at least, look nonchalant,
hanging on by my fingernails
to everything.

BY ANY OTHER NAME

'Lovely Lady'; 'Kathleen Ferrier'; 'Darcey Bussel'—you can guess
what breeders of blooms had in mind when they named these roses
though there's no hint of song or dance where they stand as upright bushes
formally arranged in rings in Queen Mary's garden in the park planned
by John Nash. I watch all the de rigeur sniffing on a sunny day as if
visitors want to inhale a whiff of fragrance, to take in a moment of time
that can only be captured in fragments. The flowers' scent is,
if not imperceptible, finely nuanced. How many shades
of rose-perfume exist ? Our olfactory sense lacks words
to attach to odours if not pungent like piss or disinfectant
or foody-smells you remember from institutions.

A walk in a park is a kind of institution; I'm struck
by colours of varying hue—
cream, yellow, apricot, red, white, black,
and more, by names that accrue
to similar arrangements of petals. Coil, spiral, whirl,
each flower's an intricate maze that stops the eye
from penetration. They don't quite come to nothing,
like a peeled onion, but, completely stripped
of its silky dressing, a rose-head atop its stem
has nothing to show but fuzz.

'Here is the 'The Royal Philharmonic', nearby the jazzy
'Jam and Jerusalem'; from 'Blue for You', 'Blessings'
'Claret', 'Garden Glory' and names of celebs.
I stop at a rose called' Perception'. Has someone signified
a rose with its own point of view? A consciousness
with no sense of self, that, perhaps, takes *us* in
by smells not from armpit or crotch
but from our individual auras
sometimes depicted by Schiele
with white lines in his paintings?

Even if we had auras would they have aromas?
If there's intelligence in us why not suppose it exists in a rose?
How wise for someone to so name one hard to distinguish
from others as if it thinks its way through the world
and celebrates
the beauty of mind.

AFTER THE CONCERT

i.m. Ray Spier and for Meri Spier

A violin's a kind of coffin
till music's played. Last night
I heard Ysaye's Poeme Elegiaque
for the first time.
A bow drawn with slow precision
closed middle movement on a note
so perfectly fused with silence—
there is no end to sound nor
beginning to utter silence

I thought, so much to be
interpreted, as when the dead,
lowered into ground or slid
through curtains into fire,
reveal a life played out
with what they've not yet said
to self or others.

My cousin, near my age,
has died. I'll miss his frequent
phone calls—arguments
on what is right or wrong
in politics, his stance
on God and science.
I'll miss his jovial voice
wishing me 'Happy Solstice'
in June and December.

This evening in the garden
I hear no cheep or chack
from birds that live around—
silence is that space
where sounds wait to be heard
and words that can't be found
in a single lifetime.

THE LANGUAGE OF LOVE

Forty set books,
all Homer and Vergil—
our tutor demanded
we master them all.

Undaunted I chose
Catullus to read
as my special text,
would not be dissuaded,

for what did I know
of corruption—words I mean,
variants to be analysed
minutely? Hard to imagine

I'd have to endure
the weekly drone
of a scholar who made
linguistic monotone

of living verse, of Lesbia.
Coming early to a row
of empty chairs, one day.
I hopped out the window

into a place unknown,
Merton Fellows' garden.
Sat there an hour before
going back to ask pardon,

and change course.
I had been naïve
wanting to study
desire and love

in a book Yet aren't they,
after all, a question of language?
Feelings and flesh suffer
from muddled verbiage—

variants of need
to be addressed,
when what one wants
can't be expressed.

O WHAT'S A PANIC IN THY BREASTIE!

That leap into the air—
hard to know who was more
shocked. Light switched on,
one small aerobatic body
in triple somersault
once and then again
couldn't find foothold
mid-air. Where was it making for,
this cartwheeling baby mouse?

Gravity won, it landed
and scurried behind the stove.
And I couldn't guess
its source of energy.
Did it hallucinate?
Had pink, powder poison
affected immature brain?
I'd asked the council officer
did mice feel pain—

when they entered
his cardboard mini-kennels.
He said they'd not squeak
nor squeal but disappear
subdued and bleed inside.
His precise craft required,
maybe, denial of rodents'
suffering— all too aware
of man's dominion

BIRD OF THE AIR

Unfocussed eyes, unpupilled, grey,
a new-born sparrow showed despair—
or did my dismay bring that look
to where it stumbled against a wall?

No hop in feet no flight in wings,
this was a bird with no future sky
nor a remembered past—his kin
a pet held on a woman's lap

to be mourned forever—
thanks to a poet. I'm no Catullus
yet lifted onto the palm of my hand
the bird throbbed like a poem wanting out

but unable to tell the all of it

QUESTION

How do they do that—change
into a rush of scent
as I come through a garden door?
How do *they,* not being gods,

metamorphise not as swans
or showers of gold but
accordion notes that go
to the heart of our inner tune

when we hear a busker?
From trains we see them alchemised
as mosaic landscapes
whose tesserae light up

from time to time in glints
of grass; like dust motes they escape—
How do the dead do that,
when they're not anywhere?

And what do they do it for?
Is it to show how absence
is breath passing as scent
in daphne and hyacinth?

THE REWARD

Instead of his son
he slaughtered a ram
trapped in a thicket.
So God let Abraham
off the hook. But rabbis,
who knew justice
had not been done,
said the ram was promised
that its kin, thereafter,
would bear sacred text
on their skin Was this
fitting reward for sacrifice—
to be flayed so God's name,
unutterable by men's lips,
could be writ on vellum?

A JEW CAN PRAY ABSURDLY

I don't believe in you;
forgive me for blaspheming;
Please exist to take control
of a world gone mad—
so my nightly prayer
when head hits pillow.

Of course, at Oxford
I became agnostic
but found at bedtime
when prayer came
I couldn't bear the conflict
between habitual heart
and new found logic.
Talking everything out
with God each night
got me through childhood.

I told a friend the prayer
that now takes hold
over reason. She laughed
and said *How very Jewish.*

I remember the tale
Jews put God on trial
at Auschwitz. The verdict
Guilty followed by
And now let's pray.

WISE MAN

(i.m. Pat de Maré)

If still alive you'd be too old
to practise psychotherapy
but I guess you'd still be playing
accordion, banjo, ukulele.

I'd be content to come to your room
to see your mantelpiece again
with its small brass buddhas
and that large photo of a nun.

I'd like to tell you last night's dream
that frightened me awake—
I'd forgotten I had to play a part
in an important play

so hadn't learned my lines.
Arriving at The Old Vic
I panicked, finding blank pages
in what should have been script

and wept out of desperation—
the show must go on…
How would you interpret this?
Left on my own I imagine

a comment about false self,
or, how I can't express
the inexpressible. You gave
always a kind of blessing,

dismissing those dreams
of missed exam or train
that my whole life through
have driven me on.

I don't now need your couch;
deep-down I hear you play
Run, rabbit run
on your ukulele.

153

THE DWARF REVISITED

A playmate of prince Baltasar Carlos, this dwarf is posed
sprawled like a child to accentuate both his stunted and
bowed legs and the fact he is not only limited in stature.
from National Gallery Exhibition Guide
18 Oct 2006–21 Jan 2007

Now let me take you round Room 4 again—
admire texture of silk and lace, see
how rapid dabs of paint anticipate
the impressionists. Velasquez made light
of sleeves and cuffs in robes grander
than Ferdinand, that rather flaccid king,
or boy-prince on a horse too big
for his boots. Now pause—Lescano's portrait.

This dwarf's composed as if the space
he takes is rightly taken, though hard to see
how and where he sits.
One leg's foreshortened, foot,
upturned, shows a large sole
on a strip of wood, part of a chair
or tree, or whatever props him up
against a swathe of green drape.

But he's no fool, is spacious,
the way he tilts his head with eyes
half-open/ half-shut weighing-up
Velasquez and appraising us
as if figuring out our size—
living the life he must
he knows he measures up.